World of
DOGS

Lara Shannon

Illustrations by Wenjia Tang

Hardie Grant
EXPLORE

Contents

Introduction

What's not to love about a dog? Those puppy-dog
eyes that melt our hearts, the boisterous energy that
keeps us on our toes and, of course, the beautiful
unconditional love that only a dog can provide.

It's no wonder dogs came to play such an important role in our
lives after they were domesticated between 15,000 and 40,000
years ago. These loyal companions provide us with affection,
protection and emotional and physical support, and they ask
for nothing more in return other than water, a meal each day, a
safe place to sleep and to be loved. Yes, the more demanding
may insist on a belly rub, a game of ball or a treat in return for
their efforts – my two, Darcy and Vindi, definitely do! But they
are our best friends, our confidants, and are often the ones we
turn to when needing a paw to lean on or our tears licked away.

While attitudes towards them differ across cultures, dogs are one of the most popular domestic animals worldwide. In *World of Dogs* you'll meet dogs from all around the globe, discover the roles dogs play in different cultures and get introduced to some fascinating new breeds.

No matter where you're from, dogs have been part of our lives for a very long time. Their appeal is universal – from featuring in Ancient Egyptian hieroglyphs to starring on the big screen (think of heroes such as Rin Tin Tin and Lassie) and becoming national treasures (like Hachikō and Balto), immortalised in statues, books and movies.

Regardless of breed, roles in history and cultural attitudes, dogs have remained our best friends for centuries. I couldn't imagine my life without them – nor would I want to.

So, let's stop chasing our tails and get on with this fabulous canine adventure.

A dog's life — from wild wolf to canine companion

.

When I wake up to my two dogs, Darcy and Vindi, patiently waiting for their morning cuddles, I often wonder how these entertaining and devoted creatures evolved from a wild animal into these playful bundles of love who vie for pole position on the bed.

While not everyone agrees exactly on when or how the dog first became domesticated, we know that they evolved from the grey wolf tens of thousands of years ago and still share 99.9 per cent of their DNA with the wolf. Looking at many of the modern dog breeds this might be hard to believe, but it's true.

Given we humans always try to make our lives easier, primitive cultures no doubt realised there were many advantages to bringing wolves into the fold: they could help with hunting, act as security guards and provide warmth and companionship. Plus, who could resist an adorable little wolf cub?

I'm sure the wolves would have seen the benefit in bonding with humans too: left-over food, shelter and the safety that being part of a pack provides, not to mention a friendly scratch behind the ear or a belly rub. A win-win situation all round. And, as soon as wolves started becoming part of a human pack, their appearance and temperaments began to adapt to their new lifestyle.

An ancient companion
The remains of a direct ancestor of today's dog were found with human remains in Bonn, Germany, buried over 14,000 years ago. It seems even back then some people were happy to have their dogs share their bed ... even the most permanent bed of all!

A dog's purpose

It was only a matter of time after dogs were domesticated (give or take a few thousand years) that humans started selecting and then cross-breeding dog types for desirable traits.

·

In the early hunter-gatherer societies, dogs were used for hunting and protection, so those that excelled in these areas continued to be chosen for their prowess. Others became herders and guardians of livestock and, before too long, dogs were being bred for many other 'jobs'.

Hounds and retrievers, with their keen sense of smell, were developed to hunt and fetch prey; shepherds and sheepdogs were bred to herd and protect livestock; and mastiffs to guard people and possessions. Sight hounds, with their long legs and agile bodies, were bred for running down prey and, later, for racing.

Some, like the early ancestors of the Cavalier King Charles Spaniel, were bred for companionship and used to warm the laps and feet of royalty and aristocrats in chilly castles and carriages. This might explain why these cuddly canines love nothing more than snuggling up with us on the couch.

The Lhasa Apso were considered good-luck charms and, along with the much loved Shih Tzu, were used as bed warmers and watchdogs in Tibetan monasteries and by holy men and nobles in China.

Believe it or not, the smallest and most ferocious of the Pekingese dogs were carried around in the robes of Chinese emperors as guard dogs and let loose on any potential threat. No wonder they still make for good little watchdogs in many homes today.

Little lions

One of the oldest dog breeds in existence,
the Pekingese were considered sacred because
of their resemblance to the lion, a symbol of
Buddha. They could only be owned by royalty,
with commoners expected to bow to the dogs.

The horse-friendly Dalmatian ran ahead of fire-fighting carriages to help clear a path through the crowds, while the Saint Bernard – a cross between the Tibetan Mastiff, Great Dane, Great Pyrenees and Greater Swiss Mountain Dog – was bred purely for rescue work in the dangerous alpine areas of Switzerland and Italy.

The Boston Terrier, known now for its good temperament, was actually bred for pit fighting – a terrible practice that sadly still goes on today. Fortunately for many dogs first bred for this purpose, such as bulldogs and staffies, they are now widely known and loved more for being faithful companion dogs.

Although some dogs still earn a dollar (well, more likely a bowl of kibble or a treat) for serving in the capacity for which they were first bred, many dogs are increasingly used for broader social purposes, such as emotional support and personal companionship. For example, Golden and Labrador Retrievers are used as seeing-eye dogs and to detect cancer, diabetes and other diseases in humans, and Beagles are great for sniffing out trouble in airports.

Canine companionship is used to encourage learning and social engagement in schools and justice systems, while therapy dogs are now widely employed in nursing homes and hospitals to lift people's spirits and help improve patient health and wellbeing.

Developing dog breeds

When it comes to 'official' dog breeds, there is no exact number, which is not surprising given how often I come across a new designer doggy name I've never heard of before. Schweenie, Morkie, Daniff, anyone?

·

The three main dog organisations across the globe have slightly different numbers:

- 195 breeds according to the American Kennel Club (AKC)

- 220 breeds according to the Kennel Club United Kingdom (KC)

- 253 breeds according to the Fédération Cynologique Internationale (aka the World Canine Association).

Leaving aside their strict protocols, though, it's estimated there are more than 350 different dog breeds in the world, and hundreds more 'species' of dogs. My two, Darcy and Vindi, fall into this mixed 'species' group given they are bits of this and bits of that, otherwise affectionately known as the 'bitzer' or 'mutt'. Let's take a look at some of the main breed groups.

HARDWORKING HERDERS

Coming in all shapes and sizes, herding dogs are hardworking and agile. They control the movement of other animals by stalking, staring down, barking or nipping, and, while this makes them sound a little mean, this group includes some of today's most popular dog breeds.

These dogs are smart and have been bred to do a job, yet now many of these backyard pooches just fulfil the roles of 'garden-bed digger-upperer', 'chief washing-on-the-line removalist' and 'fence-jumping expert' in search of some entertainment.

From the good-looking shepherds and collies, sturdy cattle dogs and corgis, to the Old English Sheepdog and the Giant Schnauzer, many herding breeds still work on the land today. Others, such as the German and Belgian Shepherds and Bouvier des Flandres, have important careers as police dogs and security guards. And it's no wonder … there's nothing like a stare or a snarl from a German Shepherd to stop you in your tracks!

Even as pets, herding dogs often revert to their instincts, rounding up their family members, particularly small children. It's also not uncommon to see cattle dogs trying to herd or nip at the heels of other dogs at the park.

A royal dog
Despite their small size, Welsh Corgis have a long history as herders and guard dogs. Queen Elizabeth II has owned and bred Pembroke Welsh Corgis since she was 18. Her corgi Monty starred with her in the opening ceremony of the 2012 London Olympics.

FAITHFUL FLOCK GUARDIANS

Large and powerful, flock guardians were first bred to guard and defend livestock such as sheep and goats. These big, beautiful breeds now protect many other vulnerable species, bonding and living closely with those under their care.

The Maremma Sheepdog, Anatolian Shepherd, Great Pyrenees, Komondor and Kangal Shepherd are known for this work today. Some even make the news (and Hollywood), such as Oddball, the Maremma Sheepdog who was tasked with guarding an island of Little Penguins in Australia, inspiring a warm-hearted movie.

It pays to be wary when approaching a flock guardian breed. While they are generally calm, they are there to protect their 'family', so best not to get too close to their 'flock'.

> These big, beautiful breeds now protect many other vulnerable species.

STUBBORN SPITZ-NORDIC

With their dense, insulated and water-resistant coats, spitz-nordic breeds evolved through the Arctic regions of the world, developed for hunting, herding and pulling sleds. Many people would not have survived Arctic conditions without the help of these dogs.

Some of the most popular breeds now kept as pets, even in some of the hottest climates in the world, include the Alaskan Malamute, Siberian Husky, Samoyed, German Spitz, Chow Chow, Keeshond, Shiba Inu and Akita.

These breeds are known for being independent and stubborn. As a dog trainer I've had my fair share of battles of the wills with these breeds and can confirm that firm leadership and good training are a must!

Summer haircare

Many people mistakenly shave the coats of these breeds during summer thinking it will help keep them cool. However, it is the thick undercoat that should be 'raked' out to keep them cool. The outer coat should be left to help circulate the air.

SLIM SIGHT HOUNDS

Generally lean and tall with long legs, a slim frame and a long, narrow head, sight hounds primarily use their keen eyesight for hunting and were selectively bred to hunt specific prey. It's no wonder they have a strong instinct to chase small animals.

On the flip side, sight hounds also have a reputation for being quiet, reserved and good with children and other dogs if socialised early.

Sight hounds include the Saluki and Greyhound, both used and bred for racing. I grew up with Greyhounds and have always loved their gentle, laidback nature.

Other big softies include the Scottish Deerhound and Irish Wolfhound, and then there's the delicate Italian Greyhound, Borzoi and Whippet (according to his DNA, my Darcy is 10 per cent whippet, so no wonder he's so fast!).

Who's the fastest?

While the Greyhound is credited as the fasted dog breed in the world, running up to 70 kilometres (45 miles) an hour, the Saluki, possibly the oldest known breed of the domesticated dog, has shown to be faster over longer distances.

SNIFFING SCENT HOUNDS

Dogs just love to sniff and smell the world (and other dogs' butts) around them, and none more so than the scent hound.

With their extensive nasal tissue and long, floppy ears that channel the scent to the nose, these hounds use their scenting ability, energy and stamina to find and wear down game.

Believed to have originated in medieval France, they have been bred to work closely with humans, so make great companion dogs (though you may struggle with their recall – their ability to reliably come when called – in the great outdoors should they find themselves on an enticing scent trail).

Scent hounds widely kept as pets include the Dachshund, Beagle, American and English Foxhounds, Basset Hound, Bloodhound and Rhodesian Ridgeback (which happens to be classified as a sight hound *and* a mastiff, so is clearly a dog of many talents).

Beagle stars

The Beagle has dominated the world of entertainment for decades. Loveable Beagle Snoopy from the comic strip *Peanuts* (and more TV specials and movies than you can count) has been around since 1950, and Brains the Beagle was the canine companion of Inspector Gadget. And who can forget Gromit, Wallace's loyal companion who also happens to like playing chess and reading the newspaper – as you can almost imagine Beagles doing.

MAGNIFICENT MASTIFFS

One of the largest breeds of dogs, mastiffs, with their muscular build and big head, were originally bred for fighting and guarding, and evolved from the Molossus dogs of Ancient Greece. Temperaments do vary between breeds but they are often stubborn and strong willed, so require firm leadership.

The Newfoundland, Bernese Mountain Dog and Dogue de Bordeaux are known for being gentle giants and wonderful family dogs (despite looking like they could eat you in one gulp), while the Rottweiler and Doberman are still commonly used as security guards – you definitely don't want to mess with these guys at work. Other popular mastiffs include the burly Bulldog, the giant Great Dane and the excitable Boxer.

TENACIOUS TERRIERS

Terriers are a tough, alert and agile bunch, originally bred in the United Kingdom and often named after the regions they came from.

The long and the short of it

Those terriers with smaller legs, such as the Norfolk, Yorkshire, West Highland and Scottish Terriers, were bred for hunting small burrowing animals and catching rats. To see the much-loved Jack Russell 'ratting' is nothing short of impressive.

Those with longer legs, such as the Irish, Wheaten, Welsh, Bedlington and Airedale Terriers, were used for hunting above ground and for guarding work.

Mixing it up

Crosses between terriers and bulldogs became popular in the 19th century, producing the powerful Bull Terrier, American Pit Bull Terrier and Staffordshire Bull Terrier, originally bred for dog fighting and bull baiting. These dogs are often considered part of the mastiff breed group as well.

Intelligent and generally cheerful and affectionate, terriers make excellent companions and watchdogs, but need training, early socialisation with other dogs and plenty of exercise thanks to their boundless energy.

GALLIVANTING GUNDOGS

With the advent of firearms, 'gundog' breeds were developed for specific hunting tasks and make up some of the world's most popular breeds (as well as a few you may never have heard of).

Pointers and setters

True to their names, pointers freeze and align their nose, body and tail to point to the prey, while setters crouch or 'set'.

The friendly English Pointer is often featured in hunting portraits from way back in history, and is still widely used in hunting and field trials in the United States and the United Kingdom today. They are also known for being gentle and loyal family pets.

The elegant English Setter is the oldest of the setter dogs, dating back at least 400 years, while the glamorous Red Irish Setter came along later and is an exuberant and affectionate companion. Setters love nothing more than getting out and about, running and chasing birds, so make sure you work on your recall!

Reliable retrievers

It's all well and good to have a dog that can point to the prey or even one that can entice it out, but most handy is one that will actually go and get it for you. That's where the retriever breeds come in, specifically bred to retrieve waterfowl using their soft mouths and ability to quickly learn not to damage the goods.

The most well-known retrievers are the Golden Retriever and Labrador Retriever, both among the most popular pet dogs and valued service animals, used for assistance and therapy work through to all kinds of scent detection roles.

Top dogs

Presidential pals of the Labrador variety include Buddy and Seamus, the pets of former American President Bill Clinton; Konni, the dog of Russian President Vladimir Putin; and Sully H.W. Bush, who served former American President George H.W. Bush during the last six months of Bush's life.

Spunky spaniels

Spaniels are a much-loved home and hunting companion, with the primary role of flushing out game or waterbirds into the line of fire, and then often retrieving them.

They include the popular English Cocker Spaniel and English Springer Spaniel, with their silky coats and long ears; their American, German and Welsh counterparts; and the Brittany and lesser-known Barbet and Pont-Audemer Spaniels. Pont-Audemer Spaniels almost became extinct (possibly because their hunting skills, best for marsh and water environments, are too specialised), despite being amusing, happy dogs with the nickname 'the little clown of the marshes'.

Crime fighters

While they may have been bred for hunting, English Springer Spaniels are often employed as sniffer dogs to detect drugs, explosives, money and people. Their acute sense of smell and impressive speed mean that, if you see one of these guys making a beeline for you at Customs, you could be in a bit of trouble.

Water-loving workers

From the Irish and American Water Spaniels and the Portuguese, French, Spanish and Frisian Water Dogs to the Nova Scotia Duck Tolling Retriever and the Lagotto Romagnolo, many of the flushing and retrieving gundogs have purpose-bred flat or curly water-resistant coats.

The immensely popular and frisky Poodle was originally bred as a water dog. Hard to believe, isn't it, given that their regal prance and coiffed hairdos suggest they have never worked a day in their life! More on the oodles of poodles later.

The multitaskers

Some gundogs are adept at multitasking, impressively able to perform all the functions of pointing, flushing and retrieving game. These include the beautiful Weimaraner, German Pointer and Hungarian Vizsla, some of the most popular hunting and companion dogs in the world. If you're after a great running, hiking or cycling mate, these are the dogs for you.

PRIMITIVE POOCHES

Also known as pariah dogs (because they were usually half-wild, outcast and ownerless), these primitive dog breeds are still closely related to an early ancestral species of dog and evolved without being part of a human 'pack'.

Most derive from either North Africa or South Asia and remain alert, independent, aloof and often difficult to predict and train.

Some of these primitive breeds kept as pets today include the Basenji, Canaan Dog, Peruvian and Mexican Hairless Dogs and the Australian Dingo. But, if you are considering one of these breeds as a pet, be prepared to have your work cut out for you – they definitely have a mind of their own.

Primitive traits

Most primitive dogs come into season only once a year, rather than twice a year like other domestic dogs. They also tend to howl, rather than bark.

TINY TOYS AND CUDDLY COMPANIONS

Many breeds in this group are much smaller versions of working dog breeds and have evolved specifically for the role of companion, with no function other than to give warmth, provide company, look decorative and entertain their owners (which sound like perfectly reasonable functions to me!).

It's no surprise then that they are (generally) exuberant and friendly and love attention.

Appearance has always mattered in the breeding of companion dogs, with selective breeding over centuries focusing purely on visual appeal. This has resulted in human-like flat faces or large round eyes as seen in popular breeds such as the Pug, French Bulldog and Cavalier King Charles Spaniel; in extravagantly long coats like those of the Maltese, Lhasa Apso and Shih Tzu; and in the almost hairless or tufted hair types like the Chinese Crested Dog.

It's no surprise then that they are (generally) exuberant and friendly and love attention, although some (think Pomeranian and Toy Poodle) can take being the centre of attention a little too far and can become very territorial, taking over the home and even their owner.

Poodles in puddles

While often referred to as the 'French poodle', it is likely the Poodle was first bred in Germany. The name 'poodle' actually derives from the German words 'pudel', which means puddle, and 'pudeln', meaning to play or splash in water.

Good things come in small packages

The chihuahua is the smallest dog breed in the world, named after the Mexican state where it was discovered in the mid-1800s, and is now one of the most popular breeds.

The most famous chihuahuas were Gidget, who rose to fame in Taco Bell ads, and Moonie, who played Bruiser Woods in *Legally Blonde 1* and *2*. Owned by the same trainer, Gidget and Moonie lived together (Gidget also acted as Bruiser Woods's mother in *Legally Blonde 2*).

The modern designer dog

The desire for designer dogs seems to have been insatiable since the early 1800s when the practice of breeding dogs for companionship rather than tasks first began. That's when the beauty contest started, sometimes causing health issues as a result.

The popular Pug is one such example. In the 19th century, Pugs had longer muzzles, long legs and more muscle, and they were less square. Now with their short noses and flat faces, they join the French Bulldog and other 'brachycephalic' breeds with a long list of major health issues.

Those with extra-long backs, like the Dachshund, are susceptible to back injuries and spinal disorders, while the hugely popular Cavalier King Charles Spaniel has a high risk of both a debilitating neurological disorder where the brain is too large for the skull and a serious heart condition.

With dogs now seen as fashion accessories in many parts of the word, the growing obsession with 'designer dogs' has many people paying exorbitant price tags and ordering dog traits and breeds as if from a fast-food menu.

Think of the 'teacup' breeds, who are bred to fit in a handbag but can end up with poor health and high anxiety levels. Or the popular Poodle crosses, desired for their curly, so called 'hypoallergenic' coats.

Designer dogs with craftily creative labels are popping up everywhere, such as the Pugalier (Pug and Cavalier King Charles Spaniel), the Puggle (Pug and Beagle) and the Shepsky (German Shepherd and Siberian Husky Cross) to name just a few.

Hairy times

Sorry to burst the bubble, but there is no such thing as a totally hypoallergenic dog breed. While some individual dogs may shed less or cause fewer allergy symptoms than others, the real source of pet allergies is often a protein that's in the saliva and urine of dogs and cats.

Dogs around the world

.

Although I haven't rounded them all up to count,
there are about 900 million dogs on Earth. The
highest numbers are found in Asia followed by
Africa. A large majority of dogs live as strays, or
are used only as guards, labour or sometimes food.
Mostly, though, we consider dogs to be one of our
closest companions, with over 470 million kept
as pets in the world.

Let's take a look at where some of our most popular
breeds came from, and discover some unique dogs
you may never have seen or heard of before.

Asia

.

This expansive continent might well
have been the first place dogs were
domesticated – this theory arose
because dogs here show the greatest
genetic diversity. Certainly, the many
vibrant cultures of Asia are home to
some fascinating dog breeds.

Japan

In Japan there are more pets than children, so it's no wonder that an entire floor of the Palette Town Mall in Tokyo's Odaiba district is dedicated to dogs. From doggy day-spas where your pet can get a massage and 'pet-i-cure', to dog-friendly cafes, canine couture and more, this incredible place fulfils a dog lover's every whim. Word has it that you can even rent a dog for a walk if you are missing some canine company while travelling (or you can visit one of the many 'dog cafes' throughout Japan). Clearly the Japanese revere the dog and the country has a couple of beautiful breeds.

.

HOKKAIDO

Also known as the Ainu-ken, Seta and Ainu dog, the Hokkaido is believed to be the oldest of the Japanese breeds and is seldom seen outside the country. In 1937 it was designated a 'rare species protected by law' and a 'Japanese Natural Monument'.

Clearly the Japanese revere the dog.

AKITA

The Japanese Akita, also known as Akita Inu, is considered a national treasure. In the past, you had to be a member of the imperial family or their court to own one. For centuries they have been the object of myth and legend and are a symbol of good luck. When a child is born, the parents usually receive an Akita figurine signifying happiness and a long life.

Developed for fighting and hunting, they are alert, intelligent and courageous. Naturally wary of strangers, they are extremely loyal and protective of their family, particularly children. One of the most famously loyal Akita of all time was Hachikō (read more about him on p. 122).

SHIBA INU

A hunting dog originally bred to flush birds and small game, the Shiba Inu is a small, alert and agile dog with a bold and spirited personality. With their pricked ears, squinty eyes, red hair, white markings and curly tail, they definitely resemble a fox.

You'll find the breed featured across the World Wide Web thanks to the ubiquitous 'Doge' meme that features the startled face of a Shiba Inu named Kabosu.

They don't bark much but are known for the 'Shiba scream' – a blood-curdling scream that rivals Jamie Lee Curtis in the classic 1978 horror film *Halloween*.

China

China has long been associated with dog-meat consumption; recently, however, the Chinese government introduced a draft policy to ban the raising of dogs for meat, recognising the sharp increase in people keeping dogs as pets, concern over animal welfare and a decline in dog-meat consumption in most parts of the country.

SHAR PEI

While most of us worry about deepening wrinkles, funnily enough when it comes to the Shar Pei it's a case of the more wrinkles the better.

Originating from southern China, the Shar Pei was bred by the ancient Chinese to guard the royal palace. The breed was kept for herding and guarding livestock, hunting and fighting, and its wrinkled skin, bristly coat, snub nose and small pointy ears were all designed to protect it in dog fights.

After a hefty tax was put on dogs in the 1940s, the Shar Pei was nearly driven to the point of extinction, leading to the *Guinness Book of World Records* naming it the rarest dog breed in the world in the late 1960s and 1970s. Their friendly temperament and compact size make Shar Peis a good companion pet, despite their permanent scowl.

PUG

You only have to scroll through your Insta or Facebook feed to see that Pugs are seriously popular pets, with their expressive faces and cheeky personalities also earning them a starring role in many a meme.

Originating somewhere in the Far East, they can be traced way back to the 1st century BCE, where they were bred as companions for ruling families in China, highly valued by Chinese emperors, kept in luxury and even guarded by soldiers!

A short and generally stocky breed (okay, I'm being tactful – many Pugs could definitely lose a few kilos), Pugs come in three colours: silver with a black face, apricot-fawn with a black face, or all black. Their appearance has changed radically over centuries, and they are now known for their wrinkled, flat faces and big round eyes that can cause them breathing and eye issues.

CHOW CHOW

Chow Chows can be traced back at least 2000 years, and were originally bred for hunting birds, guarding livestock and pulling sleds in the winter. It's hard to believe that these adorable puff balls were also raised to be sources of meat and fur.

With a sturdy build and extremely dense fur, particularly around the neck (making them look like a lion), their Chinese name is Songshi Quan, which translates to 'puffy lion dog'. They were prized by emperors and acted as models for the stone lions guarding Buddhist temples (much safer to work with a Chow Chow than a lion!). They were given the name Chow Chow in England in the late 18th century.

Freudian assistant

Working alongside the world-renowned founder of psychoanalysis, Sigmund Freud, a Chow Chow named Jo-Fi became the first-ever official canine-therapy dog. Jo-Fi helped to calm Freud's patients, especially children, and would provide insight into their mental state by staying close to depressed clients and moving away from tense ones.

India

India's colourful streets are home to roughly 35 million stray dogs, mostly native breeds like the Indian Pariah Dog and the Rajapalayam Hound. Despite dogs having a deep meaning in Hindu mythology and being worshipped in many parts of the country there is limited funding for animal welfare in India.

.

MUDHOL HOUND

If you have never heard of the Mudhol Hound, that may be because it has a multitude of other names. It's known across India as the Maratha Hound, Pashmi Hound and the Karwani Hound, meaning Caravan Hound – the British gave it this name because they thought the dog had arrived with groups (or caravans) of settlers from Asia.

The Mudhol Hound is an ancient sight hound breed, a direct descendant of the Saluki, and has served both royalty and peasants alike for centuries as guard dogs and hunting dogs. They can run almost as fast as a leopard and can leap nearly as far too.

BAKHARWAL

Another dog with many names, the Bakharwal was originally bred by the nomadic Gujjar and Bakharwal peoples to protect their livestock from predators. Today, it is also used by the Indian army.

A powerful, heavy-boned, medium-to-large-sized dog, the Bakharwal is an agile and sturdy breed, with a furry coat and a plumy tail that gives it a majestic look. As a pet food nutritionist, I am surprised that they are known to prefer a vegetarian diet of bread and milk – I'm totally flummoxed as to where they get their essential amino acids from!

You've got mail

In 2005 India Post brought out postage stamps featuring four of the country's native breeds: the Rajapalayam, Mudhol and Rampur Hounds, and the Himalayan Sheepdog.

Thailand

If you've ever been to Bangkok, I'm sure you'll have come across at least one friendly stray dog, given the city has nearly 300,000 street dogs.

Thailand is known for its stray dogs. Called soi dogs ('soi' means street in Thai), most are descendants of the native Thai Ridgeback, but many have bred with other European breeds too. The Soi Dog Foundation, based in Phuket, is a not-for-profit organisation that has helped pressure governments to ban the dog-meat trade.

.

THAI RIDGEBACK

While common in Thailand, the Thai Ridgeback is rare in other parts of the world (it's estimated there are no more than about a thousand outside Thailand).

A primitive dog breed dating back at least 3000 years, it has several traits shared by primitive breeds, such as pointed muzzles, erect ears, long, curved tails and almond-shaped eyes, much like wolves.

The Thai Ridgeback is a muscular, agile medium-sized dog. Also known as Mah Thai Lang Ahn, it was officially recognised as a breed by the American Kennel Club in the mid-1990s.

It is one of only three breeds that has a ridge of hair running along its back in the opposite direction to the rest of its coat – the others are the Rhodesian Ridgeback (*see* p. 47) and Vietnam's Phu Quoc Ridgeback.

> The Thai Ridgeback is a muscular, agile medium-sized dog.

Korea

As kooky and cute as the latest K-pop
super group, Korean dog breeds are some
of the most unique breeds in the world, and
include the Jindo, Jeju Dog, Nureongi,
Donggyeongi, Sapsali and Pungsan Dog.

JINDO

Originating on South Korea's Jindu Island, the Jindo is celebrated for its strong loyalty and bravery, and you'll find statues on the island honouring the breed.

As a Korean National Treasure, they are protected under the Cultural Properties Protection Act and even have their own dedicated research institution, the Korean Jindo Dog Research Institute.

A double-coated spitz-type dog, Jindos are known to be apprehensive and fearful of water and can easily, and I must say impressively, jump any fence under 1.8 metres (6 feet)!

Far from home

In 1993 a Jindo named Baekgu was sold by her elderly owner to a new owner more than 300 kilometres (180 miles) away. Escaping her new home, Baekgu bravely journeyed to find her way home, finally returning to her original owner seven months later, exhausted and near death. Never asked to leave home again, she lived her remaining seven years with her original elderly owner. This story of deep loyalty is so popular in South Korea that it has inspired cartoons, a TV documentary and a children's book.

Indonesia

In Indonesia only about 16 per cent of the population owns dogs as pets. But the country does have a significant number of stray dogs, and you'll find of dogs roaming the streets both in cities and regional areas. The dog-meat trade is also still of concern here, as dog meat is easy to purchase despite it being illegal to sell dog meat as food.

In recent years, many have called for an end to the trade and consumption of dog meat and the Dog Meat Free Indonesia public campaign continues to grow.

.

KINTAMANI

The Indonesian island of Bali is a place of stunning beaches and lush jungles and also thousands of confident street dogs who act like they own the place and somehow nearly always manage to adeptly step out of the way of the scooters whizzing by.

In Bali you'll also notice that many Balinese have pet dogs that look like a mix between a Samoyed and a Malamute. This rather good-looking canine is the Kintamani, or the Kintamani-Bali Dog. Native to Bali, it was developed from the free-roaming local Bali street dogs and is the only official dog breed of Indonesia, recognised by the Fédération Cynologique Internationale in 2019.

Africa and the Middle East

.

After the dog's domestication, most likely in
Central Asia at least 15,000 years ago, dogs
spread quickly to the Middle East where they
bred with Middle Eastern wolves. This new type
of dog, known as the Middle Eastern Village
Dog, was central to canine evolution, with some
migrating to Africa and developing into African
village dogs, Basenjis and other African breeds.

Those that stayed in the Middle East evolved to
become lean and long-legged, better suited to
the desert heat. These dogs led to the Canaan
Dog, an ancient type of dog that still exists
today, as well as to breeds such as the Afghan
Hound and the Saluki.

Africa

Africa is home to a number of majestic and unique animal species, so its dogs are often forgotten. Just like the continent's other animals, dog breeds vary greatly here, with some becoming popular around the world, while others still largely exist only in Africa. Interestingly, genomic evidence now suggests that some dogs in Africa descended from the jackal, rather than the wolf.

AFRICAN WILD DOG

Frequently confused with the hyena, the African Wild Dog is prided for its hunting technique and the social hierarchy within the pack. It's not in fact a dog, nor is it related to the wolf, but I wanted to include it here as they are sadly facing extinction, with less than 5000 left on the planet.

The African Wild Dog is also known as the African Painted Dog due to its spotted red, black, brown, white and yellow patches of fur. No two dogs have the same markings on their coat (each coat is entirely original, just like a human fingerprint), and they only have four toes on each foot.

> No two dogs have the same markings on their coat.

ABYSSINIAN SAND TERRIER

An old and rare breed of hairless African dog, the Abyssinian Sand Terrier has practically no hair on its body, except for a few tufts on its head and tail. They have bat-like ears, their body is sleek and their tail twisted.

The Abyssinian Sand Terrier is brave and loyal, and was often kept for comfort and to warm the bed during winter.

SLOUGHI

Revered by the Berber and Bedouin nomad tribes of North Africa and the Middle East, the Sloughi was one of their most prized possessions. Sloughis are so highly revered that a mummified body of what was thought to be a Sloughi was discovered in an Ancient Egyptian tomb. An athletic sight hound breed with an abundance of lean muscle and an elegant, wedge-shaped head, the Sloughi was bred for hunting, a role it continues to fulfil.

BASENJI

One of the most primitive dog breeds, Africa's 'Barkless Dog' is a small and skilled hunting dog, and has developed intelligence, courage and adaptability. Images of the Basenji have been found in Ancient Egyptian artefacts (likely to have been gifted from Central Africa) and in Mesopotamian art.

The Basenji can't bark like a normal dog because its larynx is unusually shaped. They make up for it by growling and making a sound somewhere between a chortle and a yodel.

A feline canine

If you're a cat person, this is the dog for you. Basenjis don't have the typical doggy smell as they groom themselves in the same way that cats do. They are also independent and aloof, much like cats too!

RHODESIAN RIDGEBACK

The Rhodesian Ridgeback is known as the African Lion Hound for a very good reason. It was developed in South Africa by Boer farmers who needed a dog to help hunt big prey – the dog had to be able to chase and corner game; cope with extreme heat, little water and rough terrain; and also fit into the family. That's quite a brief!

By crossing European dogs with a half-wild native dog breed, the farmers developed the Rhodesian Ridgeback (the half-wild native dog was excellent at hunting and had a ridge of hair along its back).

Now famous for that distinctive ridge on their short, shiny coat, Ridgebacks are also known for their love of food. If you let them eat as much as they like, they will eat until they literally make themselves sick, so watch their meal portions!

Egypt

Although there is disagreement about where dogs were first domesticated, some believe it was actually the Ancient Egyptians who domesticated dogs: a tomb dating back to 3500 BCE featured a painting of a man walking a dog on a leash. You'll find that many of today's most popular dog breeds trace back to Ancient Egypt, such as the Greyhound, Ibizan Hound, Pharaoh Hound, Saluki and Whippet.

.

Dogs in Iran

We're so used to pampering our pooches and treating them as part of the family that sometimes we forget that not everyone views dogs in the same way. In early 2019 public dog-walking was made illegal in Iran's capital, Tehran, and other strict restrictions were introduced as part of a long-standing campaign against dog ownership. The new rules were said to be needed because dogs create 'distress' among the general public.

SALUKI

Possibly the oldest known breed of domesticated dog, the beautiful Saluki has been a thing of wonder for thousands of years. They were favourites of Egyptian pharaohs and of Alexander the Great. Considered a gift from Allah, they featured on many Middle Eastern artefacts from tomb paintings to mosaic sculptures.

With their slim build and long, slender legs, they are possibly the fastest dog in the world over long distances. Salukis are quiet and gentle, but they are serious hunters at heart and phenomenal jumpers.

Israel

The second-oldest known dog remains were found in Israel (the first were in Germany), where dogs have been loved by — and buried with — humans for thousands of years.

Ahead of its Kelaviv Dog Festival, which launched in 2016 and is named for the Hebrew word for dog ('kelev') combined with Tel Aviv, Israel's capital Tel Aviv declared itself the friendliest world city for dogs. Here you'll find the most dogs per capita — dogs crowd the streets and are allowed in most cafes, stores and high-end restaurants, as well as on buses, trains and taxis. You'll also commonly see people taking their dogs to work. Now that's my kind of city!

•

CANAAN DOG

The Canaan Dog, also known as the Bedouin Sheepdog and Palestinian Pariah Dog, is a primitive dog breed that has existed for thousands of years. A rare breed, there are only about 1600 of these dogs in the world.

Depicted on tombs dated between 2200 and 2000 BCE, the Canaan Dog was used in ancient times as a watchdog and herder. Its strong protective instincts, high intelligence and watchful, inquisitive nature make it perfect for these uses to this day.

There are only about 1600 of these dogs in the world.

Europe

·

Europeans *love* their dogs, there's simply no denying it. From the elegant fluffballs accompanying their glamorous owners down Parisian lanes to the gruff Saint Bernards keeping people safe in the Swiss Alps, dogs are *everywhere* in Europe.

The continent actually played a major role in the dog's evolution — many of our favourite dog breeds were developed here. It really took off during the Victorian era, when dogs began to be bred solely for their looks and companionship, rather than a functional purpose. To be fair, I suppose looking good and warming laps do have their purpose.

Malta

Malta is a haven for canines and they are welcome in most places, including restaurants, public transport and shops. They can even be carried into supermarkets ... and why not, I say!

.

MALTESE

The Maltese is an ancient breed, one of several small Bichon dogs that have existed in the Mediterranean for thousands of years. Though the exact place of origin is a mystery, most historians pinpoint Malta for the development of the Maltese breed.

The Maltese is a toy dog covered in long, silky, white hair. Apparently Roman emperors particularly favoured this in breeding because white showed 'divinity' (clearly their dogs didn't romp in the mud like mine do!). The coat is straight and falls all the way to the floor if you don't trim it (you'll need to be keen on brushing!).

PHARAOH HOUND

This striking hound is the national dog of Malta. A descendant of Egyptian hounds, it was thought to be extinct until found in Malta.

The Pharaoh Hound has large, erect ears and was bred for hunting rabbits; with the long slender legs and body of a sight hound, they certainly love to chase prey.

A unique feature of the Pharaoh Hound – they blush when excited – was captured in an Egyptian inscription from about 1200 BCE, which read: 'The red, long-tailed dog goes at night into the stalls of the hills. He makes no delay in hunting, his face glows like a God and delights to do his work.'

> Most historians pinpoint Malta for the development of the Maltese breed.

Italy

Of Italian pet owners, around 60 per cent have dogs, which means there are around 7 million dogs in the country. In the bustling cities, you'll find them hanging out in cafes with their espresso-sipping owners, while their country counterparts will be earning their keep on the land.

·

CIRNECO DELL'ETNA

The Cirneco dell'Etna (pronounced 'cheer-*neck*-oh del et-na') is a sleek and sinewy ancient sight hound of Sicily and an athletic hunter of small game, particularly rabbits.

A purebred, the Cirneco dell'Etna goes by many names (Sicilian Greyhound and Sicilian Rabbit Hound among them) and a clue to its origin is in 'Cirneco', which derives from a Greek word meaning 'dog of Cyrene', an Ancient Greek city near modern-day Libya.

The breed is usually no taller than about 40–50 centimetres (15–20 inches) and is often described as a smaller version of the Pharaoh Hound.

CANE CORSO

Originating nearly a thousand years ago in the Tibetan highlands, the muscular Cane Corso guarded ancient monasteries. It seems the Romans were so impressed with the breed's abilities that they brought the dog back to Rome.

It's a very large mastiff and was bred to be a hunter and protector – its hunting abilities were so outstanding that it was even used to fight lions and other wild animals in Ancient Roman arenas.

The breed declined in the 20th century but dog fanciers worked to reintroduce the breed and the Cane Corso remains popular in Italy today.

Spain

Spanish dogs may be pampered but, unlike in many other parts of Europe, they are rarely welcome inside restaurants and shops in major cities, and forget about taking a large dog on public transport (only small dogs in carriers are afforded this luxury).

Thankfully, there are always exceptions to the rule: the tourist-popular Bilbao and San Sebastián are particularly dog-friendly places and you can happily dine out at your local pintxos bar with your furry friend. Keep an eye out for stickers that say, 'Perros Bienvenidos', because you and your dog will be welcome!

.

IBIZAN HOUND

This faithful and even-tempered sight hound breed dates as far back as 3400 BCE and is the dog most often represented in Egyptian art (it was even found on Tutankhamun's tomb).

Medium-sized and finely built, it can be short-coated or wirehaired and has pointy ears like many of the other ancient sight hounds – some of the wirehair types may even be found sporting a moustache!

Originally bred to hunt rabbits and small game on the Balearic island of Ibiza, these high-energy dogs are known as world-class sprinters and leapers, so keep that in mind if you decide to get one as a pet.

Bilbao and San Sebastián are particularly dog-friendly places.

BIENVENIDOS

Switzerland

When it comes to dog friendliness, Switzerland is right up there: dogs can enter most restaurants and you'll find plenty of dog-friendly hotels. What I love most about Switzerland and dogs, though, is that, if you plan on acquiring a dog, you must take a four-hour theory class on the obligations and costs of dog ownership and learn about vaccinations and other legal requirements. In most regions, owners also need to participate in practical dog-training classes. As a dog trainer and behaviourist I say 'Hallelujah!' to that and recommend all countries adopt this practice — it's one sure way to make our dogs' lives (and ours) even better.

.

SAINT BERNARD

These powerful, giant-sized, legendary dogs are best known for their life-saving search and rescue abilities. Although the Saint Bernard was traditionally thought to have originated at a monastery-hospice in the Swiss Alps in the 11th century, its first verifiable appearance was around 600 years later. It's named after a famously treacherous alpine pass high up in the Alps.

Along with other several breeds originating in Switzerland including the Bernese Mountain Dog, Entlebuch and Appenzell Cattle Dogs and Greater Swiss Mountain Dog, it is thought they were created from a cross of native Alps Dogs with mastiffs that came with the Roman Army when Emperor Augustus ruled. This canine giant is known for being loving and gentle.

Legend has it that Saint Bernards carried barrels of whiskey around their necks to help warm stranded travellers, but unfortunately this is just a folk tale.

A life-saver

Barry was a Saint Bernard who lived with monks at a hospice in south-west Switzerland, helping with mountain rescues. He is thought to have rescued more than 40 people, and revived a young boy lost in ice by licking him and carrying him back to the hospice. This brave canine died in 1814 and is now preserved at the Natural History Museum of Bern.

Germany

Dog lovers have a lot to thank Germany for, as so many of our beloved breeds have come from this country (more than 50, in fact). From the hardworking German Shepherd to the tiny Dachshund and the world's tallest dog, the Great Dane, many German dogs are purebreds. In this country, dog owners value dog training highly, so dogs here are often well behaved and welcomed in many places.

GERMAN SHEPHERD

One of the most popular breeds round the world, the German Shepherd (Deutsche Schäferhund) is a relatively modern breed of dog, developed by a German cavalry captain in the late 1800s. For a few decades of the 20th century, the breed's official name was changed to the Alsatian until it was changed back in 1977.

Heralded for their guarding and tracking abilities, German Shepherds are employed worldwide by police and armed forces for search and rescue, and drug and explosives detection work.

The most famous German Shepherd is Rin Tin Tin, who was rescued from a World War I battlefield before heading to Hollywood to star in 28 films (*see* p. 115).

DACHSHUND

Affectionately known as the Sausage Dog (as well as the Doxie, Hotdog or Wiener Dog), the Dachshund can be traced back 600 years and is a classic canine symbol of Germany.

It was developed with short legs and a long body specifically to hunt ground-dwelling animals such as badgers (its name means 'badger dog'). The modern-day Dachshund has even shorter legs than its ancestors; the two 'official' sizes are standard and miniature, but there is also a toy version.

These brave and loyal dogs are known for their bark and their stubbornness; if they catch a scent during a walk with you, good luck calling them back (make sure you have an extra special treat on hand for these times).

DOBERMAN

Given his risky job back in the late 19th century, tax collector and night watchman Karl Doberman developed the Doberman breed as a guardian dog for his protection (handily for him, he also looked after the town's dog pound). He crossbred different types of dogs, including the German Shepherd and German Pinscher, which is why the breed is called the Doberman Pinscher in some countries.

Other crosses he is thought to have used include the Rottweiler, Greyhound, Weimaraner and Manchester Terrier with the aim of creating the ideal protection dog – clearly Karl managed to do a pretty good job at it! Striking-looking dogs, Dobermans have suffered ear cropping and tail docking over the years, practices now thankfully illegal in many countries.

The United States Marine Corps used Dobermans as war dogs in World War II; the dogs were nicknamed 'devil dogs'. This probably hasn't helped their unfair reputation for being aggressive, which has more to do with upbringing and training than the breed itself. (I've known many a Doberman to be bossed around by my pint-sized Darcy.)

I've known many a Doberman to be bossed around by my pint-sized Darcy.

SCHNAUZER

The Schnauzer is a sheepdog of the Austrian Tyrol Alps region. Paintings and tapestries dating back to 1492 show dogs not unlike the modern Schnauzers, so they've been around for a while.

The word Schnauzer comes from the German word 'schnauze', meaning 'snout' and, colloquially, 'moustache', and was given to the breed because of its wonderful beard and moustache.

Originally bred to be ratters and to help out on farms, they are inquisitive, intelligent and often called 'the dog with the human brain'.

ROTTWEILERS

Rottweilers descend from the Molossus, a mastiff-type dog, and likely also from the Italian Mastiff. Their ancestors accompanied the Romans over the Alps, herding their livestock and protecting them from harm. Some historians suggest that, without these early Rottweilers, the Romans would never have survived their mountain journeys.

They were named after the German town of Rottweil and, during the Middle Ages, were used as herders, guards, messenger dogs and cart pullers. Industrialisation in the mid-1800s almost pushed them to extinction (they were no longer needed), but fortunately 'Rottie' lovers found Rottweilers a new purpose: they were some of the earliest police dogs and served with honour in the military. Rottweilers now regularly rank in the top ten breed choices in many countries.

POODLE

I have placed the poodle between Germany and France for good reason: even though the Poodle is the national dog of France, it actually originated in Germany.

The Poodle, bred as a hunting dog, was a water retriever sent to bring ducks and other birds back to their masters. The standard Poodle remains closest to these roots, but now the breed also comes as toy, miniature and medium.

Intelligent, energetic and eager to please, the smaller versions have always been companion dogs. They were highly popular in the French court during the reigns of Louis XIV and Louis XVI and also a favourite of Spanish royalty, before entering England in the 18th century and the United States in the late 19th century.

The term French Poodle is also a misnomer: in France the breed is called Caniche (derived from the French words for 'duck dog').

Poodle style

As Poodles do not shed hair, they require regular grooms (around every six weeks), which can result in many having a very fancy 'do' – some parts are shaved for cleanliness and others left long to keep organs warm and protect their legs.

France

Wander through the marvellous cities of France and you'll see just how much the French cherish their dogs. Dogs are an integral part of the French lifestyle, accompanying their humans everywhere. Even shops that serve food welcome a coiffed pooch with open arms and big smiles.

.

DOGUE DE BORDEAUX

French dog breeds are some of the oldest breeds in the world. They have been owned by everyone from French royalty to American presidents. The oldest is the Dogue de Bordeaux (Mastiff of Bordeaux) known in France as early as the 14th century, particularly around Bordeaux (hence its name).

Characterised by a massive head, a muscular body and a solemn expression on their deeply wrinkled face, they were hugely popular as hunting dogs for the 18th-century aristocracy. The Dogue de Bordeaux, despite its size and hunting talents, is a gentle giant and a much loved family dog in many countries today (one also starred in the 1989 Tom Hanks film *Turner & Hooch*).

BRIARD

This large, lively French breed is still used in France as a herder and guarder of sheep. Briards were first depicted in the 8th century during the time of Charlemagne (aka Charles the Great) where tapestries featured the king with large Briard-type dogs. Napoleon was said to have owned Briards too.

The breed's working ability was so valued that they were drafted for service in World War I, which almost caused the breed to become extinct.

Known as non-shedders, Briards have a long, thick coat that is very high maintenance and needs a *lot* of grooming, so be prepared!

BASSET HOUND

Famous as the symbol of the Hush Puppies shoe brand, the Basset Hound originated in 6th-century France as a hunting cousin to the longer-legged Bloodhound. In fact, their powerful sense of smell is second only to the Bloodhound's, and their long ears help to move smells up towards the nose, while that droopy skin on the face holds smells close.

Despite their low-slung frame, these hefty little hounds can weigh up to 30 kilograms (70 pounds).

United Kingdom
and Ireland

.

When there are dogs living it up in Buckingham
Palace, you know canines have a special place in
British culture. Some of the world's most popular
dog breeds were produced in the United Kingdom,
with aristocrats and royalty taking to dog ownership
and breeding with great gusto. Even today, Queen
Elizabeth II is renowned for her love of Welsh Corgis
and has owned more than 30 of them since
becoming queen.

The United Kingdom's Kennel Club is the oldest
recognised kennel club in the world, and in Britain
dogs make popular pets, welcomed in most public
spaces and with plenty of beautiful dog parks and
open areas for exercise. In the cold, grey winter,
though, a coat and some booties to keep their feet
toasty warm won't go astray!

England

England was home to the first official dog show;
held in 1859, it was a charity event organised by
aristocrats and brought together a huge international
community of dog lovers. Over 30 breeds originate
from England, from hunting dogs and companion
dogs to guard dogs and sheepdogs, not to mention the
English Bulldog, the national dog of England.

CAVALIER KING CHARLES SPANIEL

With their flowing fur and soft brown eyes, it's hard to resist the
charm of the Cavalier King Charles Spaniel. The dogs get their
name from King Charles II, who was known for doting on his
spaniel dogs and allowing them to roam freely in the palace.

Nicknamed 'the Comfort Spaniel', Cavalier King Charles
Spaniels were bred to keep royal laps warm in draughty
castles and on cold carriage rides. They were also brought
into beds to attract fleas, so the dogs would be bitten instead
of their owners, who were trying to avoid the plague and
other diseases.

STAFFORDSHIRE BULL TERRIER

The Staffordshire Bull Terrier comes from the Staffordshire region of England. They were originally bred from crossing bulldogs with other terrier breeds and used for bull and bear baiting until the practice was banned in the United Kingdom in the 1830s.

Affectionally known as the English Staffy, it is a very popular breed around the world. Staffies are renowned for their courage and loyal spirit, and are loving and playful, as well as completely fearless and curious. They are strong and muscly, yet surprisingly agile and, despite the fierce appearance, they generally just want to have fun. They won't, however, back down from a challenge and this has earned them a reputation for being aggressive, which they don't deserve.

The best Christmas present

In 1985 American President Ronald Reagan gave his wife a 'Cavie', as Cavaliers are affectionately known, named Rex for Christmas. Rex's first job as 'first dog' was to turn on the Christmas lights with his paw. Rex went on to live a very decadent lifestyle fitting of a 'first dog'.

Wales

There is a wonderful Welsh folk tale about a faithful hound called Gelert, who belonged to Prince Llywelyn the Great. Gelert was the prince's favourite hunting dog but on one hunt the prince went without him. When the prince returned he was greeted by Gelert, his jaws dripping with blood. Desperately searching for — and not finding — his one-year-old son, the prince killed Gelert with his sword, only to then hear his son's cry. The prince found the young child beneath his upturned cradle and there, next to him, was a large wolf, killed by the brave Gelert. Broken hearted, the prince buried Gelert outside the castle walls where everyone could see the grave and honour his courageous fight. Every year thousands of people visit the cairn of stones said to be the grave, but in all likelihood this is a moving but mythical tale.

•

PEMBROKE WELSH CORGI

With their short legs and long bodies, the Pembroke Welsh Corgi is famous for being the breed of choice for the British royal family (it was the Queen's father, King George VI, who first introduced Corgis to the royal fold). Corgis have a long history as cattle herders and guard dogs in Wales and, despite their little legs and low body, these alert and active dogs are very agile.

Legend has it that fairies used Corgis as their steeds, so the area over a Corgi's shoulders that grows in different thickness and direction is often called the 'fairy saddle'.

Scotland

Scotland is known for many wonderful things, from stunning castles, Scotch whisky and haggis (though whether this is actually wonderful is up for debate) to some of the most popular dog breeds around the world today.

No less than 14 breeds can trace their roots back to Scotland, including the Golden Retriever, Scottish and West Highland Terriers, Rough and Smooth Collies, Border and Skye Terriers and others.

BORDER COLLIE

With a reputation as the quintessential sheepdog, the Border Collie was developed in Scotland, although almost all Border Collies descended from Old Hemp, a dog born in Northern England in 1894 who had more than 200 offspring.

The word 'collie' is a Scottish word used to describe sheepdogs, but, because the breed thrived in the region on the border of Scotland and England, it was christened the Border Collie.

Border Collies are famous for staring intensely at the flock to intimidate them and for working quickly and silently to round up sheep. They are an extremely intelligent, if not *the* most intelligent, breed of dog (their closest rival for this title is arguably the Poodle), and need a significant amount of mental and physical stimulation if kept as pets.

They are an extremely intelligent, if not *the* most intelligent, breed of dog.

Ireland

It seems I have a lot in common with the Irish — a 2016 survey found that 97 per cent of all Irish dog owners talk to their dogs and 60 per cent also use a cute 'childlike' voice when talking to their pet (who doesn't do that, I ask?). A massive 69 per cent of people surveyed also said they think a family dog is what makes a house a home, compared with 55 per cent who think children do. Dogs sure are loved in Ireland!

There are nine native Irish dogs: the Irish Wolfhound, Kerry Beagle, Irish Water Spaniel, Red Setter, Red and White Setter, Irish Terrier, Irish Glen of Imaal Terrier, Soft Coated Wheaten Terrier and Kerry Blue Terrier.

.

IRISH WOLFHOUND

The striking Irish Wolfhound is the world's tallest dog breed, and can reach up to 2 metres (7 feet) tall when standing on its hind legs.

Its name comes from the breed's original purpose – hunting. For centuries, they were reserved for royalty and the nobility and were given as gifts to Roman consuls, kings, shahs of Persia and other leaders around the world. In fact, they were so popular as gifts that exports were banned in the mid-1600s because of fears Ireland wouldn't have enough Wolfhounds and would therefore be overrun with wolves.

Despite its hunting background and imposing appearance, the Irish Wolfhound makes for a terrible guard dog because of its calm and gentle nature.

A very presidential pet

Former First Lady Lou Hoover, wife of American President Herbert Hoover, was given an Irish Wolfhound when they moved into the White House. President John F. Kennedy also had an Irish Wolfhound named Wolf. Other well-known Wolfhound owners have included playwright Edward Albee and musician Sting.

North America

.

The first domesticated dogs to be kept in the Americas were brought across from Siberia more than 10,000 years ago and were descended from the Eurasian Grey Wolves rather than being descendants of North American Wolves. However, when European settlers arrived, these early domesticated dogs were all but wiped out by the settlers' European dogs. This means that the modern American dogs loved worldwide, such as Labradors and Chihuahuas, are largely descended from these European breeds rather than the canine populations that were so much a part of Native American culture for centuries.

United States

With almost 50 per cent of American households
owning a dog, it's surprising that America isn't
considered as dog-friendly as Europe is. Of course,
there are exceptions to the rule: Los Angeles is
definitely one of the most pet-friendly cities in
the country. In LA, many hotels offer pet-sitting
services, treats and a comfy pet bed, and you can
even check your dog into the Kennel Club LAX for a
groom or spa service. As with most cities around the
world, dogs do need to be on-leash in most public
areas but are welcomed at outdoor shopping malls
and most state parks, which provide a wonderful
opportunity to go hiking with your dog.

.

CAROLINA DOG

Indigenous to the United States, the Carolina Dog is a rare, primitive dog breed relatively new to domesticity. They arrived in North America about 9000 years ago (most likely from Asia) and slowly migrated until they hit the southern United States, where they have lived in the wild for hundreds of years. You can still spot them in the wild in parts of Georgia and South Carolina.

Also called the Yellow Dog, the American Dingo, the Dixie Dingo and the Yaller, they closely resemble the Asian Pariah Dog and the Australian Dingo.

As they are still not a fully domesticated breed, they are pack dogs through and through, and can blend well into homes with multiple dogs (and humans). Best to watch them around small animals, though!

'Australian' but not Aussie

Despite their name suggesting otherwise, the Australian Shepherd dog breed originated in the western United States, not Australia, and was originally bred to herd livestock around the same time as the American 1840s gold rush.

ALASKAN MALAMUTE

A beautiful dog, the Alaskan Malamute has retained many wolf-like features and is a large, imposing spitz breed that dates back over 5000 years. They are often confused with the Siberian Husky, a relative introduced to Alaska in 1908.

Named after the Inuit Mahlemut people who bred it to pull heavy sleds over long distances as well as to hunt seals and polar bears, the Malamute is still used to haul freight, assist in polar expeditions and participate in dog sled competitions.

The Alaskan Malamute became the Alaskan state dog in 2010 thanks to a group of school kids advocating the Alaska Legislature for it as part of a class project.

Canada

We all know Canada is one of the friendliest, most welcoming countries around – and, no surprise, they welcome dogs too! Canada ranks fourth in the world's most dog-friendly countries, just behind France, Switzerland and Italy. In British Columbia, you can hit the ski slopes with your pooch (or leave them snuggled up back at the cabin) at a number of pet-friendly ski resorts. Calgary is a dog's paradise with more off-leash spaces than any other city in North America.

.

LABRADOR RETRIEVER

One of the most popular dogs around the world is the Labrador Retriever. Although the name might suggest they came from Labrador, Canada, the breed actually originated in Canada's Newfoundland in the 1830s. Small water dogs were bred with Newfoundlands to create a breed called the St John's Water Dog or Lesser Newfoundland that, with their waterproof coats, would help local fishers tow in their catches and retrieve any escaping fish. They were then bred with British hunting dogs to create what has become known as today's Labrador Retriever.

With their amazing retrieving skills and sense of smell, Labradors now help out with tracking work for police, in search and rescue roles, and in assistance work (due to their steady character). They make wonderful family dogs, but you will need to vacuum often as their short coat sure does shed! And if you go anywhere near the water, expect them to jump straight in.

As soft as ...
The adorable Labrador puppy has been part of marketing toilet paper for over 45 years, representing the Andrex toilet paper brand in Britain, the Kleenex counterpart in Australia and other brands in more than 30 other countries.

Mexico

Mexico has some ancient canine breeds like the Xolo that were revered by the Aztecs, and it is the origin of the much loved Chihuahua. But it also has a huge number of street dogs, estimated at between 15 and 18 million. The problem stems from a limited access to desexing services, which is crucial to help stop this number from rising.

XOLOITZCUINTLE

One of the most ancient dog breeds of the Americas, the Xoloitzcuintle, also known as the Xolo or Mexican hairless dog, is one of several breeds of hairless dog. It's believed that around 3500 years ago the dog's early ancestors accompanied migrants from Asia and developed into the breed seen today.

They were used as guard dogs to protect the home from evil spirits.

Ancient Aztecs named the breed for their dog-headed god Xolotl. Xolos were considered sacred by the Aztecs and were often sacrificed and buried alongside their owners to serve as protective guides to the next world. They were used as guard dogs to protect the home from evil spirits and some were sacrificed or ritually eaten at religious ceremonies (sounds like a terrible reward for being so sacred!) almost leading to their extinction.

CHIHUAHUA

It may be pint-sized but the Chihuahua sure packs a punch and is now one of the most popular breeds in the United States. Recognised as the smallest dog breed, it got its name from the Mexican state of Chihuahua, where it was first noted in the mid-19th century.

The Chihuahua is thought to have developed from the Techichi, a tiny, mute dog kept by the Toltec people of Mexico.

Relative to their bodies, Chihuahuas have the biggest brain in the dog world and can be rather fierce despite their size. In 2014 a pack of stray Chihuahuas terrorised the American town of Maryvale, forming large groups, chasing children and defecating anywhere they wanted. Bad dogs!

Latin America and the Caribbean

·

The domestic dog first arrived in South
America about 4000 years ago, travelling south
from North America. The oldest breed, the
Peruvian Hairless dog, is at least 1500 years
old, and was a favourite of the Inca Empire.
These days most of the dogs you'll find in this
part of the world are breeds that have been
recently introduced.

Panama

Large dog breeds are quite rare in Panama —
people here mostly own small dogs, which are
allowed in almost all outdoor places and even in
many businesses. Panama is also home to a rare and
unusual species of animal called the Bush Dog.

.

BUSH DOG

One of the world's most mysterious species, Bush Dogs are not much larger than a cat and Panama is the only country in Central America where the species is known to live, aside from a few unconfirmed sightings in eastern Costa Rica near the Panamanian border. Mainly living in tropical forests, they hunt in packs and communicate with a high-pitched whine.

Bush Dogs are classified as a near-threatened species by the International Union for Conservation of Nature because populations continue to decline.

Argentina

As disposable incomes rise among the middle class in Argentina, more money is being spent on pets, especially dogs. Don't be surprised to see a dog walker handling a pack as large as 20 dogs when taking to the streets of Buenos Aires — talk about a thriving business opportunity for multitasking dog lovers!

.

DOGO ARGENTINO

Also known as the Argentinian Mastiff and bred from old fighting dogs such as mastiffs and bulldogs, the Dogo Argentino is often mistaken for a Pit Bull.

This large, white, muscular breed of dog was created in the 1920s in Cordoba, Argentina, by a local doctor for the purpose of big-game hunting. He also wanted a brave dog that would protect its human companion, so they are known to be kind but can have an over-protective temperament.

Ownership of the Dogo Argentino is banned in several countries, such as the United Kingdom, Ukraine, Australia and New Zealand. Sadly, this is because their great hunting qualities meant they were often forced into dog fighting, rather than it being a reflection on the dog breed itself, which can be friendly, tolerant and affectionate with early socialisation and good leadership.

Brazil

Brazil is home to an estimated 52 million dogs —
more than anywhere else in Latin America. However,
there's a great divide in how local dogs live their lives.
In wealthy areas, dogs go to fancy shopping malls,
sit on laps in restaurants, paddle-board with their
owners and get wheeled around in strollers. In the
poorer communities, however, they live on the streets
and hunt in packs for food. This has led to dogs being
considered one of the most destructive predators in
Brazil, hunting wild and endangered prey in nature
reserves and national parks.

•

FILA BRASILEIRO

Brazil's national dog, also known as the Brazilian Mastiff, is a large working breed used for hunting, tracking and guarding livestock. Rather than attacking its prey, the Fila traps it and waits for the hunter to arrive. In the 18th century, when slavery was legal in Brazil, Brazilian Mastiffs were used to track escaped slaves and hold them until their owner arrived.

Because of their naturally protective instincts, they are considered a dangerous breed in some countries, despite being loyal and quiet in a family environment.

Peru

In the Peruvian capital, Lima, dogs are loved
and, while street dogs exist, many of the dogs
you see wandering the streets do have owners.
In Peru, its common for people to let their dogs
roam freely, and only return in the evening for
dinner and to sleep.

.

PERUVIAN HAIRLESS

The Peruvian Hairless, also called the Peruvian Inca Orchid, is a
rare purebred that has been around since the time of the Incas,
if not longer. Depictions of hairless dogs have been found on
South American pottery dating to 750 CE.

An elegant and slim dog, their distinguishing feature is
their hairlessness, though there are some born with coats.
Interestingly, the same litter can produce both coated and
hairless dogs.

Commonly seen in the homes of Inca nobility, they were
persecuted almost to extinction after the Spanish Conquest
of Peru in the 16th century but have been a protected breed
in Peru since 2001.

Cuba

More pervasive than classic 1950's American cars and colourful street art, the dog should be the national symbol of Cuba. You'll find dogs of all shapes and sizes wandering the streets of Havana. The country's warm, dry climate make it well-suited for the fluffy coat of it's national breed, the Havanese.

·

HAVANESE

Once called the Spanish Silk Poodle and the Havana Silk Dog, the Havanese originates from the ancient Bichon family of little white dogs. Bred as a companion dog for the Cuban aristocracy in the 1800s and named after Cuba's capital, they are small and clever with a thick but silky coat.

Like many of their ancestral breeds, such as the Bichon Frise and Maltese, they have been nicknamed the 'Velcro dog' because they stick so closely to their owner's side.

Famous owners of Havanese have included Barbara Walters, Venus Williams, Joan Rivers, Queen Anne, Queen Victoria, Charles Dickens and Ernest Hemingway.

Oceania

·

The dogs of Oceania — unique populations found in Australia, New Zealand and the surrounding islands — originated from East Asian dogs more than 3300 years ago.

While both Australia and New Zealand are nations of pet lovers, cultural attitudes to dogs do differ considerably in the wider Oceania region.

Australia

Australians have long had a connection with dogs. The First Nations peoples, the earliest inhabitants of the continent, tell tales of the native canine, or Dingo, as being both a feared foe and a valued companion. In current-day Australia, dogs are welcome in many places, with dedicated cafes and pet-friendly accommodation, but they still aren't welcomed the way you might see in Europe (not enough for my liking, anyway!). This is despite many Australians considering their pet a special member of the family.

A number of working dog breeds were bred in Australia and can still be seen rounding up livestock on farms across the country — examples include the Australian Cattle Dog, Kelpie and Stumpy Tail Cattle Dog. Though most of the Aussie dog breeds are a blend of other imported breeds, many of the medium to large breeds have one common thread: the Dingo.

.

DINGO

The Dingo is legendary as Australia's wild dog, though it also occurs in South-East Asia, and was introduced to the continent some 3000 to 4000 years ago.

The Dingo once inhabited many parts of Australia (except for the island state of Tasmania), but after European colonisation there was a movement to remove Dingoes from farming areas, so they are no longer found in many parts of the country. In fact, the world's largest fence was built to keep out Dingoes, and it spans 5614 kilometres (3488 miles) of the south-eastern Australian desert.

Dingoes and domestic dogs interbreed freely with each other so the term 'wild dog' is often used to describe all Dingoes, Dingo hybrids and other feral domestic dogs.

AUSTRALIAN CATTLE DOG

Also known as the Blue Heeler or Queensland Heeler, Australian Cattle Dogs are the culmination of the cross-breeding of the Blue Merle and the Australian Dingo by British arrivals in Australia in the late 1800s.

A unique, tough, hardworking dog suited to the outback, they are traditionally used to drive cattle along by nipping at their heels.

This tough breed has gained a new image – and a new following – thanks to the hugely popular animated children's TV show *Bluey*, all about a young Australian Cattle Dog and her family.

New Zealand

While dogs are still a popular pet in the Land of the Long White Cloud, cats actually rule in the ownership stakes with 45 per cent of households owning a cat and only 31 per cent owning dogs.

Cat and dog over-population, however, is negatively affecting the native fauna and environment of this magnificently scenic country, and there are calls for more desexing and animal control to help address the problem.

•

HUNTAWAY

While its exact origin is unknown, the Huntaway first appeared in written record in 1870. Bred by mixing the Border Collie with a variety of other breeds such as the Doberman, it is a unique sheep-herding dog because it uses its voice to drive the sheep.

The Huntaway is perfectly suited to New Zealand farming conditions and is a hardworking dog with great stamina and plenty of self-discipline.

Papua New Guinea and Indonesia

On this island in the South Pacific Ocean, you'll find diverse landscapes, fascinating culture and unique wildlife, such as the Singing Dog.

SINGING DOG

One of the world's rarest wild dogs, the New Guinea Highland Dog, found on the island of New Guinea, was given the alternative name of the Singing Dog as it has the ability to vary the notes of its howl, making a haunting and extraordinary sound.

Once considered to be a separate species in its own right, it is actually closely related to the Australian Dingo and is an introverted and independent animal that developed without a great deal of human interaction. They do tend to bring this attitude into the home when kept as pets.

Cultured canines

·

With the dog evolving from wild wolf
to loyal companion, it is no surprise
that dogs also began to feature in many
aspects of our culture, from art and
religion to movies and books. And now
we're seeing dogs move from the page
and screen to become huge stars on
social media!

Religion

Dogs featured on tombs, monuments and temples
around the world, and in Ancient Egypt they were
considered to possess god-like characteristics – so
much so that rulers were even buried with their
favourite dog to protect them in the afterlife
(an unfortunate fate for a favourite pet!). Other
historical evidence shows the religious significance
of dogs, including sculptures and mummified bodies
from the Mayan Classic era (approximately the
3rd–9th centuries) and Aztec pottery figures of dogs
buried with the dead in the 14th–16th centuries.

.

Today, a favourite poem for many pet owners is 'Rainbow
Bridge' (no one is sure who wrote it). It tells the story of a
wonderful place where our dogs who have died spend their
days playing in the fields waiting patiently for us to join them.
When our time comes to cross the Rainbow Bridge we will
be welcomed by our beloved pooches with wagging tails and
bountiful joy. Whenever I read this poem it always brings a tear
to my eye thinking about my own dogs who have passed and
a hope that this beautiful story is indeed true.

Art

Most of what we know about the role and domestication of the dog has been gleaned from historic art and artefacts. Cultured canines have featured in rock paintings found in ancient caves, on Greek and Roman sculptures and relics, in mosaics retrieved from the ashes of Pompeii and in medieval tapestries, including the famous Bayeux Tapestry from the 11th century, which features dogs that look like sight hounds.

.

As dog breeds and their relationship with humans evolved, dogs featured more prominently in art. Hunting scenes with dogs become popular in art from the Middle Ages and Renaissance periods, and dogs appeared in portraits with aristocrats and wealthy owners who considered them a status symbol. More recently, 20th-century artists Pablo Picasso, Andy Warhol and David Hockney all painted pictures of their dachshunds, while Jeff Koons and his sculpture *Puppy*, along with his various Balloon Dogs, made canine waves in the art world (especially when his *Balloon Dog (Orange)* sculpture sold for US$58.4 million in 2013).

Literature

Who doesn't want to read a book about a dog? We've certainly been reading about them in stories, poetry and other literature for thousands of years — *Aesop's Fables*, written in Ancient Greece during the 6th century BCE, featured at least 20 stories about dogs. And I certainly loved Enid Blyton's *Famous Five* series when I was a child, especially the little bitzer Timmy, who my own dog Darcy reminds me of.

Here are a few more dogs who have become household names and firm family favourites.

.

LASSIE

Many a Saturday was spent in our house watching *Lassie* episodes, but the story was actually based on the 1940 novel *Lassie Come Home* by Eric Knight, which tells the tale of a faithful Collie sold to another family. The Collie then takes off on an epic journey to get home and reunite with the young boy she loves.

TOTO

Another childhood favourite of many (including me) was *The Wonderful Wizard of Oz*, a classic children's book by L. Frank Baum before it became a movie. Toto, a Cairn Terrier, is Dorothy's trusty sidekick on her journey through the land of Oz.

CLIFFORD

Clifford the Big Red Dog is a children's book series by Norman Bridwell, first published in 1963, about a giant red Vizsla named Clifford. It was later turned into a television series.

OLD YELLER

Old Yeller, by Fred Gipson, was a book about a Labrador Mastiff cross who bravely protects his owners against wolves, bears and other wild animals. Spoiler alert: I remember crying my heart out at the end of this story after Old Yeller gets rabies from a wolf and has to be put down.

NANA

Peter Pan or the Boy Who Wouldn't Grow Up is a 1904 play and a 1911 novel by J.M. Barrie that features a Newfoundland named Nana who takes care of the Darling family's children. As with many of these other books, it went on to become a much loved movie.

PONGO

The Hundred and One Dalmatians is a 1956 children's novel by Dodie Smith about the adventures of Pongo, the father of 15 Dalmatian puppies stolen by fur-loving Cruella de Vil. This one has a happy ending, thankfully, with Pongo reunited with his puppies plus extras, so in the end there are 101 Dalmatians! Yet another movie success followed.

SNOWY

In the classic comic-book series *The Adventures of Tintin* by Hergé, Snowy (called 'Milou' in the original French version) is Tintin's best friend. Snowy was based on a Wire Fox Terrier and is a talking dog who loves food and whisky. Despite Snowy's preference, dogs should definitely not drink alcohol!

FANG

Fang is Hagrid's large pet dog in the *Harry Potter* book series and, despite his scary name, Fang is afraid of almost everything. Still, he finds the courage to join Harry and his fellow students on their dangerous journeys and to protect his master from threatening spells.

SNOOPY

Snoopy is a humanised Beagle who first appeared in the *Peanuts* comic strip, created by Charles M. Schultz in 1950. The beloved pooch eventually made his way onto the big screen with the rest of the *Peanuts* gang. Snoopy has become one of the most recognisable and iconic characters from the comic strip.

Film and TV

From cartoon characters to real-life dogs and canine superheroes stealing the show, dogs have been a big part of film and TV since the start of the 20th century. Here are some of the most notable canine screen-stars from past and present.

SCOOBY-DOO
My favourite cartoon show of all time, *Scooby-Doo, Where Are You!* featured the loveable talking Great Dane Scooby-Doo, who helped solve mysteries with his human gang, Shaggy, Fred, Velma and Daphne.

MR FAMOUS
A Yorkshire Terrier belonging to film star Audrey Hepburn, Mr Famous appeared alongside her in *Funny Face* in 1957.

UGGIE
A Jack Russell Terrier, Uggie was famous for numerous film roles including one in the award-winning *The Artist* in 2011.

BIG RED

This Red Setter was a champion show dog who preferred to hunt rather than prance and ultimately ran away to bigger and better things.

RIN TIN TIN

Rescued from a World War I battlefield by an American soldier, this legendary German Shepherd was taken to California and trained for film work. Starring in 28 Hollywood films, he became a fully fledged international movie star.

BEETHOVEN

First released in 1992, *Beethoven* was a movie featuring a loveable Saint Bernard called Beethoven, and his family spends the whole time trying to control his crazy antics.

CUJO

At the other end of the scale is the 1983 horror film *Cujo*, based on Stephen King's 1981 novel, featuring a Saint Bernard infected with rabies. (I lost sleep for weeks after seeing this one.)

BEASLEY

Beasley, the canine star of the 1989 comedy *Turner & Hooch*, was a Dogue de Bordeaux, a breed that surged in popularity after this film.

MARLEY

It's hard to forget the gorgeous Golden Retriever Marley, the centre of the 2008 romantic comedy *Marley & Me* starring Owen Wilson and Jennifer Aniston.

DYNAMITE DARCY

Okay, he may not be a Hollywood star or have saved lives (yet!) but, as my canine co-host of the popular Australian TV show *Pooches at Play*, Dynamite Darcy has won many fans with his tiny stature and big personality. His newly adopted brother Vindi is now set to star alongside him (and me) too. You can check them out on Instagram @dynamitedarcy.

Dynamite Darcy has won many fans with his tiny stature and big personality.

Social media

We love dogs. We love social media. So it's no surprise
that dogs are now stars of the online world.

·

Dogs have gone viral. Across the internet you'll find their
expressive faces posted, shared, and liked, in everything from
the 'Doge' meme to dog-shaming photos and videos. Online,
just like offline, dogs are a hit.

The most followed pet on social media is Jiffpom the
Pomeranian, with tens of millions of followers across his social
media channels. He's also set a couple of world records for
running on either his front or hind legs, and appeared in Katy
Perry's *Dark Horse* music video, which has been viewed nearly
three billion times on YouTube. So, he's pretty famous.

Then there is Doug the Pug. What a life this little guy has with
tens of millions of followers, a People's Choice award and an
Instagrammer of the Year award under his belt, and invitations
to numerous red-carpet events where he hangs out with
A-list celebrities.

In recent years the pet version of the modelling agency has
developed, with a growing number of animal talent agencies
popping up and promising wannabe stars the opportunity to
become the next su-paw-star!

Popular pooches

While we humans like to think of ourselves as unique and creative, when it comes to choosing a name for our dogs we have some common favourites.

·

I've sifted through the data on the most popular dog names from 16 countries and now have the definitive list of the ten most popular dog names for dogs from 2020. Drum roll please ...

Girls	Boys
Bella	Charlie
Luna	Max
Lola	Milo
Bailey	Buddy
Mollie	Jack
Ruby	Rocky
Poppy	Cooper
Daisy	Alfie
Lucy	Oscar
Maggie	Teddy

World famous dogs

.

You've just met — or been reintroduced to — famous dogs in art, literature and movies. Here are a few more well-known dogs who have been recognised for their unconditional loyalty and bravery … or just for being amazing.

HACHIKŌ THE AKITA

The most famous Akita of all time was Hachikō, who would wait at the Shibuya train station in Japan each evening for his owner, Professor Ueno, to arrive from work, then they'd walk home together. After Ueno unexpectedly died at work, Hachikō continued going to the station each day, waiting for Ueno to arrive on the train. He did this for *ten years* until his death in March 1935. Hachikō's story symbolises loyalty and fidelity for many in Japan. A statue of him can be seen at Shibuya train station and he's featured in many books and movies.

BALTO THE SIBERIAN HUSKY

During the 1925 diphtheria epidemic, relay teams of sled dogs helped to stop the disease breaking out in Nome, Alaska, by transporting the vaccine from Anchorage. Balto, a Siberian Husky, achieved fame for leading the final team through terrible blizzards to safely deliver the last batch of the vaccine. A statue of Balto was erected in Central Park, New York City, and, after he died at the age of 14, his body was mounted and donated to the Cleveland Museum of Natural History where it still remains.

GREYFRIARS BOBBY THE SKYE TERRIER

Greyfriars Bobby would keep his owner, John Gray, company on Gray's shifts as a night watchman with the Edinburgh Police Force in the 19th century. After Gray died, Bobby, a Skye Terrier, spent 14 years guarding Gray's grave until Bobby himself died on 14 January 1872, aged 16. Known as Greyfriars Bobby, a statue of Bobby can be seen at the corner of Edinburgh's Candlemaker Row and George IV Bridge.

OLD SHEP

Another tear-jerker is the story of Forever Faithful Old Shep, a dog living in the town of Fort Benton, Montana, in America. Old Shep kept a six-year vigil for his shepherd owner who had fallen ill and died. After seeing his coffin loaded on to a train, Old Shep would meet each incoming train to look for his master. In 1942 he was killed by a train and buried at the bluff overlooking the station, where a bronze statue of him can still be seen.

DOG ON THE TUCKERBOX

Located in my home country of Australia, the Dog on the Tuckerbox is a historical monument and tourist attraction in Snake Gully near Gundagai in New South Wales. Inspiration for the statue is thought to have come from the poem 'Bullocky Bill', published anonymously in 1857, about a dog sitting on or spoiling the food in the tuckerbox (a lunch box) of a bullock driver, but it's since also been celebrated in song and story. The monument was erected in 1932 to assist Gundagai Hospital and money from its wishing well is still donated to the hospital today.

SNUPPY THE WORLD'S FIRST CLONED DOG

In 2005 Snuppy, the world's first cloned dog, was revealed by the Seoul National University in South Korea. Created using DNA from the cells of an Afghan Hound's ears that were inserted into eggs from female dogs and then implanted into 123 surrogate mothers, two cloned pups were produced but only one survived: Snuppy, genetically identical to his father. A few years later Snuppy went on to father ten puppies to two cloned mothers. Mind-boggling stuff!

TUCKER BOX

PIONEER MONUMENT

GUNDAGAI

Sporting dogs

Dogs have worked alongside humans
for thousands of years, yet even in
ancient times we found ways of using
dogs for sport and entertainment.
Given their hunting origins, most
dogs love nothing more than running
and chasing prey, so some of the most
popular and enduring sports involve
racing and speed. Others can focus
on endurance, agility and obedience.
And, believe it or not, some even
involve dancing!

You'll find a growing number of novice and professional dog sports on offer around the globe that can provide many benefits to both you and your dog. For a dog, sports allow it to fulfil its innate desire, whether it be to herd, chase, scent, retrieve or more. For you, they offer a fun fitness activity and help to create greater communication and a deeper bond between the two of you.

Here are some of the most popular dog sports enjoyed around the word (jump online to find organisations and competitions near you).

OBEDIENCE TRIALS

In these trials, the dog must perfectly execute a predefined set of tasks when directed to do so by the handler. The dog is judged by its understanding and reliability in responding to commands.

AGILITY

The dog is directed through a set obstacle course within a certain time limit. Courses typically have between 14 and 20 obstacles, including tunnels, weave poles, tyre jumps, seesaws and pause tables, where the dog must stop for a set amount of time.

HERDING

Herding, also known as a sheepdog or stock dog trial, is a competitive dog sport in which herding dogs move sheep around a field, through fences and gates, and into enclosures as directed by their handlers.

FLYBALL RACING

Teams of dogs race to the finish line, over a line of hurdles, to reach a box that, when the dog presses the spring-loaded pad, releases a tennis ball. The dog has to catch the ball then race back to their handlers with it.

DISC DOG

Also commonly called 'frisbee dog', disc dog competitions involve a person throwing a disc for the dog to catch. Throwers compete in events such as distance catching and (somewhat) choreographed freestyle catching.

DOCK JUMPING

Sometimes called dock diving, dogs compete by jumping for distance or height from a dock into water, such as a lake or bay. Dock jumping is popular in the United States and you'll also find events in the United Kingdom, Australia, Germany and Austria.

LURE COURSING

Also called Greyhound racing, it involves purebred sight hound breeds chasing a mechanically operated lure.

HOUND TRIALLING

One for the scent hounds like the Beagle, Bassett, Dachshund and Coonhound, these trials challenge the hounds in terms of endurance and scenting drive. The dogs have to follow a scent track over rough terrain, sometimes working with scents that are days old.

NOSE WORK/SCENT DETECTION

In the sport of scent work, working detection dogs have to find an odour or scent and let their handler know that the scent has been found. To make it extra challenging, detection is done in a range of environments and often during tough weather conditions.

SCHUTZHUND

German for protection dog, schutzhund tests a dog's protection, obedience and tracking talents. It's currently known competitively as IGP (previously IPO) and focuses on working dogs – the tests are really about finding out if the dog has the necessary abilities to be a good working dog.

EARTHDOG TRIALS

Earthdog trials are for the short-legged dogs among us (whether they be terriers or Dachshunds or others) known for their ability to hunt small animals, particularly underground. Earthdog 'den tests' involve the dogs having to navigate human-made tunnels while scenting a rat.

RALLY OBEDIENCE

Also known as Rally or Rally-O, this is a dog sport for those obedient dogs (trust me, obedience just takes practice and training). In Rally-O, the human competitors move through a course with the dog in heel position and follow the instructions on 10 to 20 signs along the course (rather than wait for a judge's direction).

In Rally-O, the human competitors move through a course with the dog in heel position.

RETRIEVING TRIALS

These are the ideal competitions for purebred gundogs. Dogs are tested for obedience and their natural retrieving and hunting abilities in settings that imitate natural hunting situations.

SLED DOG RACING

Most popular (of course) in the Arctic regions of the Northern Hemisphere, the sport involves teams of sled dogs pulling a sled with the dog driver standing on the sled runners. The team that completes the course in the shortest time is the winner. Sledding can be done in hotter, drier climes – in Australia races occur on a dirt track.

CANICROSS

Like to run with your dog? Then canicross, the sport of cross-country running with dogs, is for you. It originated in Europe as off-season training for the sledding community, but is now a standalone sport throughout Europe and is growing in popularity in other countries such as Australia.

DOG DANCING

A relatively new dog competition for the creative ones among us, this sport, also known as 'heelwork to music', involves people dancing with their dogs to choreographed routines for four minutes (you pick the music and choreograph the dance).

Top dogs on show

AKC NATIONAL CHAMPIONSHIPS (USA)

The AKC National Championship is held by the American Kennel Club every year in December or January in the United States. Over 5000 dogs from all over the world compete, but only seven go to 'best in show'. Bourbon the Whippet triumphed over more than 4000 competitors to earn a $50,000 cash prize and the title of Best in Show at the 2020 championships.

WORLD DOG SHOW (EUROPE)

The World Dog Show, sanctioned by the Fédération Cynologique Internationale and called 'the most important dog show in the world', is a week-long international dog show, held since 1971. The World Show events include agility, obedience, junior handler and conformation, along with other events and demonstrations. The 2020 event was due to be held in Madrid, but was postponed due to COVID-19.

WESTMINSTER KENNEL CLUB DOG SHOW (USA)

The Westminster Kennel Club Dog Show, held in New York City since 1877, is an all-breed conformation show. While searching for America's top dog, the show celebrates the companionship of dogs and also promotes responsible dog ownership, dog health and breed preservation. In 2021, the event moved to Tarrytown, New York, so it could be held outdoors due to the pandemic.

CRUFTS OBEDIENCE CHAMPIONSHIPS (UK)

Celebrating its 130th anniversary in 2021, the Crufts Obedience Championships are the highlight of the British obedience calendar, when the best of British obedience dogs and their handlers compete for the title of Crufts Obedience Champion. Throughout the year there are 46 championship shows around the United Kingdom that host qualifying classes for the Crufts Obedience Championships. The Crufts 2020 Best in Show champion was Maisie the Wirehaired Dachshund from Gloucestershire.

INTERGROOM (USA)

Intergroom is an international grooming conference and competition held each year in New Jersey. As well as grooming competitions, it features an extensive seminar series with all the latest tips and techniques of interest to dog groomers and salon owners.

THE WORLD'S UGLIEST DOG CONTEST (USA)

I couldn't leave this one off the list! I believe beauty is in the eye of the beholder, and what might seem ugly to some can be beautiful to many others. And there's no better example of this than the World's Ugliest Dog Contest. An annual contest held in Petaluma, California, as part of the Sonoma-Marin Fair, it was cancelled in 2020 due to the pandemic. But in 2019 Scamp the Tramp was crowned the World's Ugliest Dog. The most notable winner, however, is Sam, a Chinese Crested who has won it three times.

About the author

As a one of Australia's most well-known dog experts and animal welfare advocates, pet behaviourist, dog trainer and TV presenter Lara Shannon is passionate about educating and empowering people to help improve the lives of companion animals.

Lara has worked in the media for the past two decades, promoting important animal conservation, pet behaviour and welfare issues. She is the producer and host of popular Australian TV show *Pooches at Play* and features in the TV series *The Pet Rescuers*.

An Ambassador for Second Chance Animal Rescue, Pets of the Homeless and the Companion Animal Rescue Awards, Lara is driven by her mission to help reduce the needless euthanasia of adoptable shelter animals down to zero.

Never far from Lara's side is the cheeky Dynamite Darcy, who Lara adopted in 2017, and her recent rescue pup, Vindi, who is flourishing in his role alongside Darcy as a canine co-host on *Pooches at Play*.

Lara's first book, *Eat, Play, Love (Your Dog)*, was published in 2020 by Hardie Grant Travel and is available where all good books are sold in Australia, USA and UK.

www.larashannon.com

About the illustrator

Wenjia Tang is a freelance illustrator who graduated from Maryland Institute College of Art in 2017. She was born in south-east China, and went to the United States for high school when she was 15. She loves all kinds of animals, and lives with a cat in Manhattan, New York.

Her work has been recognised by American Illustration, Society of Illustrators, *Communication Arts*, AOI, *3x3 Magazine* and more.

Published in 2021 by Hardie Grant Explore,
a division of Hardie Grant Publishing

Hardie Grant Explore (Melbourne)
Wurundjeri Country
Building 1, 658 Church Street
Richmond, Victoria 3121

Hardie Grant Explore (Sydney)
Gadigal Country
Level 7, 45 Jones Street
Ultimo, NSW 2007

www.hardiegrant.com/au/explore

A catalogue record for this
book is available from the
National Library of Australia

Hardie Grant acknowledges the Traditional Owners of the Country on which we
work, the Wurundjeri people of the Kulin Nation and the Gadigal people of the
Eora Nation, and recognises their continuing connection to the land, waters and
culture. We pay our respects to their Elders past, present and emerging.

World of Dogs
ISBN 9781741177725

10 9 8 7 6 5 4 3 2 1

Publisher	**Senior editor**	**Design**
Melissa Kayser	Megan Cuthbert	Michelle Mackintosh
Project editor	**Proofreader**	**Typesetting**
Alexandra Payne	Judith Bamber	Megan Ellis

Colour reproduction by Megan Ellis and Splitting Image Colour Studio
Printed and bound in China by LEO Paper Products LTD.

MIX
Paper from
responsible sources
FSC® C020056
www.fsc.org

The paper this book is printed on is certified
against the Forest Stewardship Council®
Standards and other sources. FSC® promotes
environmentally responsible, socially beneficial
and economically viable management of the
world's forests.